Reptile Life Cycles

BY BRAY JACOBSON

Gareth Stevens
PUBLISHING

CRASHCOURSE

Please visit our website, www.garethstevens.com. For a free color catalog of all our high-quality books, call toll free 1-800-542-2595 or fax 1-877-542-2596.

Cataloging-in-Publication Data

Names: Jacobson, Bray.
Title: Reptile life cycles / Bray Jacobson.
Description: New York : Gareth Stevens Publishing, 2018. | Series: A look at life cycles | Includes index.
Identifiers: ISBN 9781538210536 (pbk.) | ISBN 9781538210543 (library bound) | ISBN 9781538210529 (6 pack)
Subjects: LCSH: Reptiles--Life cycles--Juvenile literature.
Classification: LCC QL644.2 J25 2018 | DDC 597.9'156--dc23

First Edition

Published in 2018 by
Gareth Stevens Publishing
111 East 14th Street, Suite 349
New York, NY 10003

Copyright © 2018 Gareth Stevens Publishing

Designer: Samantha DeMartin
Editor: Kristen Nelson

Photo credits: Series art Im stocker/Shutterstock.com; cover, pp. 1, 5 (snake) reptiles4all/Shutterstock.com; p. 5 (crocodile) Audrey Snider-Bell/Shutterstock.com; p. 5 (turtle) Constantin Iosif/Shutterstock.com; p. 5 (tuatara) Rudmer Zwerver/Shutterstock.com; p. 7 (frill-necked lizard) Matt Cornish/Shutterstock.com; p. 7 (gavial) Lucie Placha/Shutterstock.com; p. 9 David Evison/Shutterstock.com; p. 11 WeStudio/Shutterstock.com; p. 13 Natalia Kuzmina/Shutterstock.com; p. 15 Irina oxilixo Danilova/Shutterstock.com; p. 17 Heiko Kiera/Shutterstock.com; p. 19 Paul Whitman/Science Source/Getty Images; p. 21 Vitalii Hulai/Shutterstock.com; p. 23 IrinaK/Shutterstock.com; p. 25 foryouinf/Shutterstock.com; p. 27 Shane Myers Photography/Shutterstock.com; p. 29 Andrey Armyagov/Shutterstock.com; p. 30 Rich Carey/Shutterstock.com.

Printed in the United States of America

CPSIA compliance information: Batch #CW18GS: For further information contact Gareth Stevens, New York, New York at 1-800-542-2595.

Contents

Reptiles at a Glance   4

Egg Time   8

Hatching   10

Keep Growing   12

Begin Again   14

Making Sense of Snakes   16

Swimming with Sea Turtles   22

The Life Cycle of a Sea Turtle   30

Glossary   31

For More Information   32

Index   32

Words in the glossary appear in **bold** type the first time they are used in the text.

Reptiles
at a Glance

Reptiles are animals that are **cold-blooded** and have scales covering their body for **protection**. They have backbones, too. All reptiles fit into one of four main groups: turtles, tuataras, lizards and snakes, and crocodiles.

Make the Grade

The turtle group includes tortoises. The crocodile group includes alligators, caimans, and gavials, too.

crocodile

turtle

tuatara

snake

5

There are more than 10,000 species, or kinds, of reptiles on Earth. Because there are so many different species, reptiles can look very different from one another! However, they have life cycles that are alike.

Make the Grade

A life cycle is made up of the main parts of an animal's life, beginning with its birth.

frill-necked lizard

gavial

7

Egg Time

Most reptiles begin life in an egg. The shell may be hard or leathery. Female reptiles often lay their eggs near water or in soil that's a bit wet. They commonly dig a hole to bury the eggs in or lay them underground.

Make the Grade

Reptile eggs are buried so they can **incubate**. How long they incubate depends on the reptile species.

green turtle
eggs

9

Hatching

Reptiles use a special body part called an egg tooth to hatch, or break out of, their egg. These babies are now called hatchlings. Most often, they take care of themselves soon after hatching. Some mothers, such as crocodiles, guard their hatchlings, though.

Make the Grade

An egg's temperature controls whether the baby will be male or female! In turtles, lower temperatures make female babies and higher temperatures make males.

baby crocodile

Keep Growing

Young reptiles, called juveniles, look like small adults. They have to eat well and stay away from predators to grow to their full size. How long this takes depends on the species! Snakes called boa constrictors take years to reach full size.

Make the Grade

Boa constrictors are less than 2 feet (0.6 m) long at birth and can grow to be more than 10 feet (3 m)!

13

Begin Again

Once fully grown, reptiles are commonly ready to find a mate, or another animal of its kind to produce babies with. They're going to start the life cycle all over again!

Make the Grade

While the main steps of the reptile life cycle are the same, each species has **adapted** it to the conditions around it.

The Reptile Life Cycle

egg

adult

hatchling

juvenile

Making Sense of Snakes

Some snakes begin their life cycle a little differently from other reptiles. Most snakes do hatch from eggs, but not all hatch in an underground nest. Some snake eggs hatch inside their mother's body! Then, the mother gives birth to live babies.

Make the Grade

Snake hatchlings are sometimes called snakelets.

Other kinds of snakes don't hatch from eggs at all! Instead, the baby snakes simply grow inside their mother. Water snakes and some kinds of boas are snakes that **reproduce** this way.

Make the Grade

Animals that have babies growing inside their mother, but not inside an egg, are called viviparous.

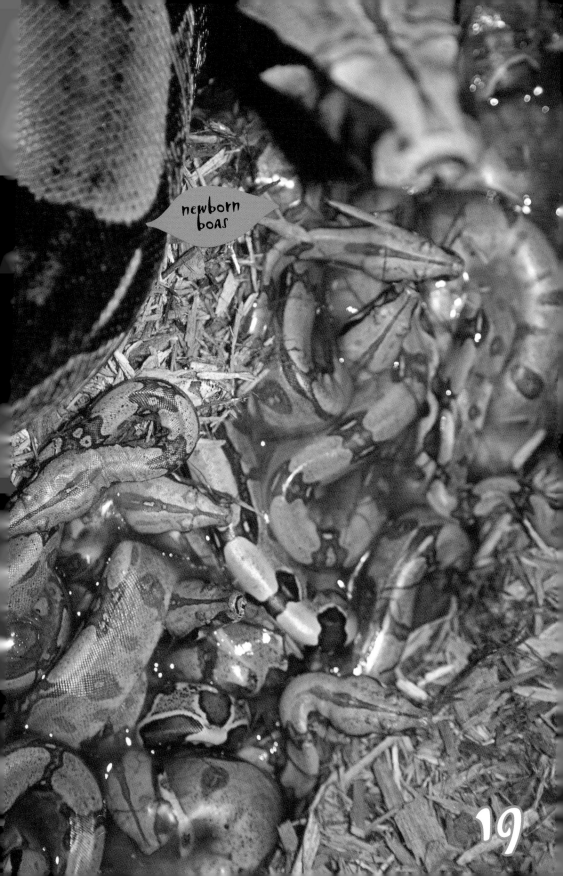

newborn boas

19

As juvenile snakes grow, they **shed** their skin. That's because as they grow, their skin doesn't grow with them! Adult snakes shed, too, but not as often. Snakes commonly shed their skin all in one piece!

Make the Grade

All reptiles shed their skin! Lizards shed just a bit at a time.

The Life Cycle of a Grass Snake

Adult male and female snakes mate.

Female snake lays eggs.

Juvenile snakes shed their skin as they grow.

Snakelets hatch.

Swimming with Sea Turtles

When a mother sea turtle is ready to lay eggs, she heads to the beach. She buries her eggs in a hole in the sand. About 6 to 8 weeks later, her babies hatch, climb to the surface, and head to the ocean.

Make the Grade

Sea turtles lay their eggs on **tropical** beaches all over the world.

23

Many baby sea turtles don't make it to the ocean because of predators and human **interference**. Hatchlings that do make it to their first swim may not return to the coast until about 10 years later. These juveniles are looking to eat!

Make the Grade

Scientists don't know much about the first 10 years of a sea turtle's life except that it lives and grows in the open ocean.

25

When a sea turtle is fully grown depends on the kind of sea turtle. It may take as long as 50 years for sea turtles to be ready to mate! Sea turtles **migrate** long distances to find their mates in special **breeding** areas.

Make the Grade

Sea turtles in the wild may live as long as 100 years!

27

Some species of sea turtles make several nests of eggs. They lay about 100 eggs at a time! Once a mother sea turtle has laid all her eggs, she heads back into the ocean. She will likely mate again in 2 to 3 years.

Make the Grade

A group of sea turtle eggs is called a clutch.

The Life Cycle of a Sea Turtle

Mother sea turtles lay eggs in a hole in the sand.

Sea turtles hatch and crawl to the ocean.

Male and female sea turtles mate.

Hatchlings grow in the open ocean for about 10 years.

Once fully grown, sea turtles migrate to breeding areas.

Juvenile sea turtles return to the coast to feed.

Glossary

adapt: to change to suit conditions

breeding: mating and giving birth

cold-blooded: having a body temperature that's the same as the temperature of the surroundings

incubate: to keep eggs warm so they can hatch

interference: the act of getting in the way

migrate: to move from one area to another for feeding or having babies

protection: having to do with keeping safe

reproduce: when an animal creates another creature just like itself

shed: to lose a body covering, such as skin

tropical: having to do with the warm parts of Earth near the equator

For More Information

Books

Midthun, Joseph. *Animal Life Cycles*. Chicago, IL: World Book, 2014.

Riehecky, Janet. *Reptiles*. North Mankato, MN: Capstone Press, 2017.

Websites

Life Cycles

mos.org/sites/dev-elvis.mos.org/files/docs/education/mos_life-cycles_reptile.pdf

Use this colorful PDF to review the life cycles of many kinds of animals.

Index

adults 12, 13, 20, 21
egg tooth 10
eggs 8, 10, 11, 15, 16, 18, 21, 22, 28, 30
female 8, 11, 21, 30
hatch 10, 16, 18, 20, 22, 30

hatchlings 10, 15, 16, 24, 30
incubate 8
juveniles 12, 15, 20, 21, 24, 30
live babies 16
male 11, 21, 30
mate 14, 21, 26, 28, 30

placenta 18
shed 20, 21
viviparous 18